ا ا (ا) اسید رشیبار
مع خیسا ستات
ا ا ا
ل ل سا لعل ه
ا
سب

TO FINBARR
with all my
Respect .
Jim
17/10/

Nostalgia

by

Ali Hussein

ORIGINAL WRITING

ISBN: 978-1-907179-21-1

A CIP catalogue for this book is available from the National Library.

Published by Original Writing Ltd., Dublin, 2009.

Printed in Great Britain by the MPG Books Group, Bodmin and King's Lynn

To my wife Arina the inspiration
The back bone and
The motivation for this book to see
"The light"

Dedication

For the soul of my father in the heavens of the Lord,
The man who taught me how to walk tall.
To my mothers prayers that protect me from those who envy.
To those who run in their veins some of my blood.
To Benghazi the forgotten city
That gave me the meaning of belonging.
To Dublin for it's kindness.
To my friends on the road to Nostalgia
To Sarah Magee for being always there,
To Altrhouni acknowledgement of my gratitude.
To Sofyan the light of my life and the reason I pray to
stay a little longer.
To all of you I give you my humble poetry.

I petty those who indict and hurt people with false allegations and indulge themselves in such inequity. I will remain as I do - a giant walking among giants, arming myself with the only weapons at my disposal -veracity, virtue, and vigilance, for me they are indispensable.

"After climbing one hill, one only finds that there are many more hills to climb"

Nelson Mandela

Contents

Nostalgia

"All that lives must die, passing through nature to eternity"

William Shakespeare

ENTER

It's Smokey and hard to breath
Just like conflagration
Continuously grasping for air
Always seems like I'm taking my last breath
Surrounded by ugly shapes
And shadows of death
Madness and books of sadness
Sweet sorrows of the prophets
Fighting falsehood
Along with the lord
With mighty sword
We call it the Word
So come in my majesty
My queen of happiness
Enter my soul and through
My eyes
Discover the world

2009

"He dares to be a fool, and that is the first step in the direction of wisdom"

James Huneker

JASMINE

Alone,
My glass and flickering lights.
Blonds,
Brunettes and long summer nights.
Champagne,
Light heads and red carpet.
The sun stole the moon and took
Her to new orbit.
Waiting, but my trains
Are always late.
Dreaming of home but
Between us
Is an iron gate.
Devil pretends to be saint,
High-class hookers,
Easy bait.
Swinging trays,
Caviar in golden plates,
Funny images,
Horrible fate.
Empty souls,
Paper mate.

Hate to love
Love to hate.
Hundred drinks,
Bruised liver,
Wounded heart.
Turned my head, I saw the moon
Looking great
Would you like to be my date?
Took me by the hand,
Walk me down
To lonely street,
Danced with mid night moon
Until the break of dawn.
I felt the breeze
Cooling my head
From long summer heat
Coiled body
In a city park seat.
Alone,
Another night,
Dimmed light,
Second exile,
Long lonely mile,
Hundred drinks
To sooth the pain.
One question:
"Will she ever make it, Jasmine?"

June 97

4

"By three methods we may learn wisdom, first by reflection, which is noblest. Second by imitation, which is easiest, and third by experience, which is the bitterest?"

Confucius

ANOTHER READING IN THE BOOK OF SADNESS

1

I always wanted to
write something
No one ever wrote before.
I knocked at the gates of
wisdom
and with the keys of knowledge,
I opened a million doors.
Just to learn
that my soul bleeds with pain,
a poem is born.
Like a child, I wrote it on the
Walls with a chalk.
It's washed away by the rain,
I start talking to myself.
They start whispering, "He's mad".
They took me away from my sanity,
and I try to write it once again,
I become sad.

2

I have a name
A thousand years old
and a heart of gold.
A civilization that reached
China Wall and gone
beyond the land of the Mongol.
Now the world rules with the law
of the jungle.
The devils gamble on the world
with a game of "poker".
Who was once the king is now the joker.

Now I am a prisoner inside a circle
and because of my belief
I've been singled out.
I'm Sinbad wandering in the sea
For thousands of years,
dreaming of Baghdad
and a safer shore.
So my ship can finally land.
Every time I think I become sad.

3

My heart is suspended
 Like a cloud between two skies,
Torn between two cities
should I choose the winds
that travels to the west
where my love is?
Or should I send my cloud with
the winds that travel east
where my childhood friends,
the blue waters,
My mother's face
and the golden sun are?
Every time I ask myself
To the West or to the East?
I become sad.

4

Sad is my voice will reach you through the
wire
and will make the gap wider
and higher.
Tears will fall like a running
river.
Anger in my eyes and
the heart is burning like blazing
fire.
Mayhem will rule in the absence
of the law-giver.
Lies, double standards and hypocrisy
will make the soul shiver.
The truthful will be
condemned and millions of
the brain-washed
will gather around the liar.
It's mad,
every time I come closer to the truth
I become deeply sad.

October 1990

"Those who whisper falsehood suffer from a disease called insecurity"

Ali Hussein

DON'T KILL

Don't kill inside me the
feelings and the sensation
for the things I love most.
Don't kill my feelings towards
the trees, the pigeons
and the rain,
Don't kill my love to
the rivers, the perfume,
the beauty and The Lord.
Without these feelings
I'm hopeless and lost.
Don't kill my feelings towards friendship,
childhood and love,
They are my prison
that I seek no freedom
don't ask me why,
don't ask me the
reason.
Let me submerge
beneath my tears
Leave me to my
loneliness,
let me crucify my soul
between your nipples
alone, let me face my fears.

March 1996

"I deserted the world and sought solitude because I became tired of rendering courtesy to those multitudes who believe that humility, is a sort of weakness and mercy a kind of cowardice, and snobbery a form of strength"

Gibran.K.Gibran

DRUMS

They will come like ice,
Lightning, thunder and rain.
They will come through the keyhole,
they will put fear in the hearts,
they will terrify the souls,
they will come through the letterbox
the tap and the drains.
Singing, they will come
with the rattlesnake,
they will come dancing
on the African drum.
They will come from a faraway land
creeping like the desert sand.
They will come with the ocean waves;
they will pop out from the graves.
They will come like Death
to silence the tongue
and take away the breath.
They will come
from above, soaring,
they will come
from the left roaring,
from the right
they will come howling.
from underneath
they come crawling.
The blind will see them,

the deaf will hear them
the mute will talk to them
and the king will die.
With a knight and a rook
his throne will fall
along with his Falk.
For thousands of years they will rule,
they will conquer
From where the sunset
and the rise of the moon,
their long awaiting baby
will be born
a thousand years
before
The Lord claims the earth
on the break of dawn.

July 2005

"Genuine poetry can communicate before it's understood"

T.S.Elliot

LETTER IN A BOTTLE

On August 20th the "Kursk"- one of the aging Russian nuclear submarines, was hit by a foreign object, which is still a mystery up to this day, started to sink and continued to sink till it hit the ocean bed, 100 metres deep. It had one hundred and eighteen crew. All the crew died but Yuri was one of the last to die. He made it to the hatch for one last bid to open it, even though he knew he will be dead if he manages to open it but it is the last hope that gives us the power to stay alive. Yuri managed to write a small note to his love - Olga. He shoved the letter into an empty bottle of vodka before he took his last breath. The bottle floated in the submarine till it found an escape route. It took a journey of three months to land in the shores of Malahide. As I was taking the stroll, thinking about the people whom I left behind long ago, hoping they are still hopeful as I am. I found Yuri's bottle to Olga and this is what it said:

I am alone
I feel lonely
I am disconnected
Isolated and
Totally submerged
My dear Olga,
As I am taking my
Last breath,
I smell nothing
But the horrible death.
Yuri, Sergey and Nikolay

Have just faded away
Holding each other's hands,
Dreaming of a blue sky
And a piece of land.

How is it, my Olga
Up there?
I miss you,
I miss my home,
I miss the snow.
I can only say
Now: ljublju, ljublju
What can I tell you?
About down here
But the ultimate fear
Loneliness,
Sadness,
Tears,
And no one near.
Me and my captain,
Vladimir, we have
made it to the hatch
calling, " Pull me, lad
death is near and
sooner will snatch."
My hands are bleeding
I can hear him shouting,
"Well done."

It was silence
oh my God
He is gone.

Oh, how hard it is
my Olga to die
alone.
And the sorrow
is cutting deep
through the
bone.
No loving hands
to hold.
And no soft voice
coming through
The phone to tell you,
"Privet,
Kak dela?
Horosho.
Ljublju, ljublju[1] ."

Was it big news?
Mayhem
And great fuss,
or they kept it
a secret and
No one must know?
If that is the case

[1] privet, kak dela, horosho, liublju" are Russian words for "greetings, how are you? good and I love you."

What a horrible way to go.

Did they perform the death march?
Did they play
The sad pipe?
Did they fire the farewell
salute?
Or all went mute
And hush, hush, hush?

Did they tell you
I died brave?
When I was hopeless
Let down
Powerless
And will never
Have a head stone.
Nor grave.
Good bye,
my Olga, it's time
For me to go.
Oh it's horrible the
Death that crawls
So slow.

Its silence and
So dark just like
The ocean floor
I feel like a prisoner

To a death cell
That has no door.
I think of you,
My home,
The air
And a safe shore.

Remember me
Every time your
Eyes meet the ocean
And think that every wave
Is a kiss
Coming to you
From my "Kursk"
Grave.
Think of me
Every time it rains
And my Olga
Have no sorrow
Have no pain.
Yuri.

I sighed and my heart cried as I remember the people behind those great waters - my family, my home and my friends. I shoved the letter back into the bottle and sent it back to the great ocean; hoping one day it will find Olga and Olga will find the truth.

August 2003

LOLITA
(To a woman from the Baltic's)

Lolita sleeps all day,
Dreaming of the men who escape the
gates of the morning.
The pains of the heart,
The noisy city and its fast tracks.
Lolita touches the peaches
on her naked chest,
Wriggles like the grass snake and
opens her eyes with the sunset.
Lolita stands in front of her mirror,
Thousands of butterflies
Lands on her dresser to rest.
Lolita puts on her French perfume;
pairs of swans land to nest,
thousands of honeybees
surround her, lured by her scent.
Lolita with ten lotus flowers
puts on her sexy black tights
touches the soul.
She steals away the seconds and
The time crucifies the pendulum on the wall.

Lolita puts on her dress,
Thousands of red roses bloom,
the almond trees blossom,
Fields of jasmine and heather grow;

Lolita loves to walk bare footed,
like the stones, the sand grains,
The rivers and the children.
When Lolita walks, it follows her
The queen bees, the cuckoos and the whydah.
The sky opens its doors
to bless the ground that she walks
with soft, drizzly rain.
To "love" Lolita knows a million paths,
Knows how to change sadness into mirth.
Lolita cries in silence like the chrysanthemum
of the wounded earth.
Lolita weeps like the weeping of the grass
in the moment of dying.
Lolita - a mix of winter and summer fruits.
Lolita is the balance between the evil and good.
Lolita drinks her red wine
and talks about her spoiled childhood.
Lolita lights up a cigarette and speaks about
the hunting dogs, the opera nights,
the unforgettable symphonies
And the French food.
Takes drag from her cigarette,
blows circles of smoke and with her finger
draws a woman in the nude.
She recites Yevgeny's poetry,
Speaks about the suffering of "Nietzsche",
the waiting for Godot and
The sweet memories.

She drinks more until her lips
take the colour of strawberry.
Lolita is a beautiful contradiction,
Lolita - words of perfection.

Oh come near, Lolita - my priceless tear,
sing to me, Lolita, a Russian song.
Sing till I dissolve my soul in your soul,
sometimes sing with mirth,
Sometimes sing with grief and moan.
Sing to me till the morning star;
sing to me till the break of dawn.
Let me suck the sweetness
of wine from your lips, let me bury my head
between your nipples, let me relax a little from
my papers, my poetry and my ink.
Let me put aside my tired quill,
close my eyes and take a break
from the endless dip.

Let me walk you with my hands around
your shoulder and sometimes
with my hands around your hips.
Let me Lolita lean on you,
Let your heart to be my pillow,
Let me search for you in you,
Let me shed some leaves from the tree
of my eternal sorrow.
Let me keep distance and

Sometimes let me be your shadow,
let me practice with you

The naughtiness of the children
let me draw you with coal.
Let me paint you sometimes with colour,
let me dive to touch the
Depth of your soul let me understand
the concept of demise and birth.
Let me once live the joy of the mirth.
Lolita is a cold breeze in a hot summer's day,
Lolita - pure like the dew of the dawn,
new like the waters of the river.
I beg you, Lolita, with the things you love
to be merciful with my heart and forever stay.
Lolita walks like the peacock -
Vain and proud.

Lolita steals a hundred hearts
with a glance and turn to steal
another hundred on the other side.
Lolita is the shortest road between
Earth and Heavens.
My favourite number, the day I was born
seventh of the seven.
Without Lolita I will live in darkness
like the mole.
I fear the time, that one day
they will steal away your eyes,

your face and your soul.
I fear the fishermen that one day they will
steal my beautiful shell, the sea,
the shores and the sand.
I fear the painters will steal
My drawing book,
The colour's case, the brush and the stand.
I fear the poets will steal my favourite poem,
leaving me broken and sad.
Lolita - academy for beautiful arts,
school that teaches love and
nurses the wounded hearts.
Lolita fields of opium, lilies
and chrysanthemum.

Lolita is the sweetness of the honey
under the tongue,
The oxygen that burns inside my lung.
Lolita, you are my whistle,
You are my hum and my
favourite song.
Come nearer to my heart,
touch my sorrow
Keep tighter and the distance narrow.

July 2002.

"I have wept but you didn't cry, I have sung but you didn't dance"

Gibran.K.Gibran

MALONE

Every time I hear your name,
my sweet Molly Malone,
I remember Dublin,
I remember Joyce and I remember the tragedy
of the wild salmon
 I think of their suicidal journey
because they are
Like you and I, my friend
we love the river.
Every time I hear the voice of the singer
telling the sad story of yours,
my memory squeezes me,
I drip with pain, sad pictures flashes
before my eyes and I see rain.
I see places I have never seen before.
I see a house I have never opened or closed its door.
Corners, but I can't see the friend of yesterday.
Suddenly I grow older and
My hair turns to grey,
I hear the cracking of your wheel-barrow
I see you, I see the fish basket
I look at your face,
I see sorrow.

You are wet like a cat
And the skies of Dublin have no mercy.
Its clouds forever rain

I look at your face again,
I see a picture painted with the colour of pain
your hands shaking like a leaf in a windy day,
your body is wasted
And fading away.
Oh, Malone only if you knew
That winter in Dublin and the hardship
will leave you with the remains of a beautiful girl.
It's the wicked fever, my little pearl.
She passed before my eyes,
Like time passes through the universe
wondered away like the end of a sad song
my heart was torn between the joys when
the earth gives birth and the snatching
of loved ones by the horrible death.
I'm isolated like a worshiper in his dome
hopeless like a ship fighting a storm.
Lived my life dancing on the edge of the sword
and own nothing in this world
but a pencil, my sadness and a mighty word
so will you remember me, Malone?
Suddenly she stopped and the world
submerged in silence.
Towards me she walked to narrow the distance,
leaned across my shoulder with a heavenly whisper.
In painful departure she left me in a state of sombre
and Dublin sleeps in a glass of pain,
Waking to the truth that
Molly will never be back again.

Every time winter passes through Dublin
the ghostly shadow of a beautiful girl
appears till the morning star and the
break of dawn.
Pushing her wheel-barrow
In a bony frame and face full of sorrow.
Every time I hear your name whisper in my ear
It echoes across the universe and it lingers and lingers.
Every time I hear your name,
I cry for you, my sweet Malone
I cry for Dublin,
I cry for the tragedy of the wild salmon.

May 1990.

"Homes are like suitcases, we carry them wherever we go"

Ali Hussein

NOSTALGIC

Another winter passes through my soul.
My heart still longing for home
From the beginning of this river
until the end of the storm
The legs are slowing, my hair turning grey
I remember when I kissed my
Mum "Good-bye".
Alone in Dublin the city that lives.
Outside the circle of moment, where the old,
Counting their days with cups of teas and sips of beer.
I was alone and felt like a wounded deer
In Grafton Street all the faces
Seemed so beautiful
With eyes of empty stare
December passing through the soul
Cutting deep through the bone
My feet felt like stone.
My head was invaded with memories of now and rare.
I walked until the morning star,
Second exile, another death, long lonely mile.
One question: "Where to and how far"?
I was alone
And home in my heart, home in my heart,
home in my heart.

Dublin 1990.

*"I pray you pull back your cavalry and leave
this matter to me"*

Saladin

Nothing

Nothing,
but empty bottles,
broken glasses
and loneliness.
Nothing but walking alone.
The sorrow, cutting deep
through the bone.
Hearts of stone,
empty mailbox,
dead phone,
lonely stars
and crying moon.
Nothing but sadness that
running deep through the vein.
Exceedingly growing
beyond the borders
of the pain.
Nothing but shuttered dreams,
broken promises,
funny shapes.
Lifeless paints
in golden frames.
Shallow minds and
sour grapes, faked smiles,
masked faces
and sadness.

Nothing but ugly faces
behind beautiful masks.
Poison lips of deadly serpents,
fatal kisses and madness.
Nothing but circular journey,
endless lap
broken bridges
hard to gap.
Dangerous roads with a million traps.
One gives with hand of mercy
a thousand greedy souls ready to grab.
Crossroads in wasteland
With no compass, no maps.
Nothing but deadly silence,
dripping tap, nuisance flies,
sleepless eyes desperate for nap
and sadness.
Nothing but false tears
of lifeless eyes, mean souls,
hungry mouths, dying child,
crying hearts.
Open wounds and big lies.
Nothing but words no deeds.
Foes, no mates,
closing gates, hocks, no bait
Lovers, no dates, God, but no faith
one dies of hunger
Another eats from a golden plate.

Fast tracks, but always late.
Nothing but fighting for one god
Same god
Horribly bad
Deeply sad
Totally mad
All claim the gates of heavens
Blindly walking
Falsely driven
Instead of love, hate were given
Alive but not living.

Nothing but, speculation
Presumption,
Assumption,
And lies,
I hold the truth
My ultimate freedom, it's mine.
The darkness shall be defeated, by the morning sunshine
The masks will fall
The ugly souls will crumble
And the world will be just fine.

October 2006.

"Sorrow is the language of the soul"

Ali Hussein

Sadness of the moon

Sad, is the moon
Because of the ugliness that occurs
Deep under the wings of darkness
to suppress and demise
and conspire to put out
your light that shines in my eyes.
Sad, is the moon from those who dig at nigh
To change the path of the river.
And those who want to put out the
light of God with their mouths by
Speaking lies.
I will share your sadness till the end of days
So be kind and draw a smile on your face.

Dublin 1990.

"I can forgive Alfred Noble for having invented dynamite, but only a fiend in human form could have invented the noble prize"

G.B. Shaw

SHAME
(To Abeer, speaking beyond the grave)

Fourteen years of age,
Innocent child, raped, humiliated by
a heavily armed American soldier.
He stole her pride
Immoral, empty mind
cold eyes of dead fish
heartless and snitch
He pulls his trouser up,
He picks up his heavy-duty machine gun
from the edge of her bed,
He emptied two bullets
in her parent's heads.
For him it was a little fun,
no conscience, no guilt.
He turns his head towards her
to see if he inflicted more hurt.
She looks at him
like he was nothing but dirt.
He says with heavy accent
"Did you enjoy that, you little brat?
Look at me, remember my face,
remember my name - It's John Wayne."
Tell me: "Can you feel the pain?"
He screams at her
Like he is insane:
"You Arab Muslim bastard,

I will blow your brains out!"
She tells him in
Arabic, with a fearful voice,
"You are nothing but a mole.
Falsely driven, empty soul,
black heart the colour of coal,
You are nothing but a sad fool.
You look at me, remember my face
It will live inside your head, engraved on its wall.
I will try to forgive and forget
You have to live with that.

My wounded heart will heal soon,
my soul will cope with its pain
I will wash my sadness
with the dew of the dawn,
I will wash your shame with heavenly rain.
Soon you will have children
Of your own like I was, they will be
innocent and full of grace.
But Wayne, you will never have peace
because every time you look at them
you will see my face.
You murdered the sun and the moon,
You turned my world into darkness;
you have made me an orphan, sad and alone.
Go now, leave me to my grief and moan.
I will grow stronger and weaker you will grow.
I will live beyond my death, you will be forgotten,

your death will be painfully slow. Go home,
you have no business here; you came, you destroy,
you turn my country into "State of fear".
Go, let me dream of Aladdin, the fairytales
and the city of Baghdad, let me sit by the window;
let me wait for the return of my Sinbad.
Go, give me time to grieve for Mama and Dad,
and give me time to whisper to the skies,
Let me speak to The Lord with the voice of silence,
let me ask a couple of questions,
Let me try to understand.
Go home, let me be alone like a Sufi in my little dome,
let me ascend with my soul above my pain
Don't make me grow quick.
Let me dream of babies,
let me dream of knights and white horses,
let me play with my friend's bride and groom.
Give me space, give me room, go to Mama before
the storm, I will defeat your darkness,
I will light a little candle, I will become pure and humble,
I will live brave and simple.
You can't deny me, you can't break me
so what's your gain?
I will live, you will die, soldier Wayne."

April 2006.

This is the true story of a young Iraqi girl who was brutally raped then shot
dead along with her mum, dad and her six year old sister by an American
soldier.

"Pray that your loneliness may spur you into something to live for, great enough to die for"

Dag Hammarskjold

SIGH

In her eyes
he saw a lost soul and touch of
fear.
With a heavy sigh said:
"Men do cry".
She closed the curtain
on her "ocean blue" eyes
to hide her tear.
The grass cries, the trees,
the wind and the sea
but men don't cry.
Rebecca cried under
the influence of cocaine and beer.
Oh, Rebecca, come near
talk to me about the
loneliness of the soul,
talk to me about the rivers of the pain,
let your heart erupt
the volcano of rage,
Let it burn the wasteland of our age;
let us tear the book of sadness,
page by page.
Then let it rain, let it rain,
let me engrave you
eternal tear on my cheek
then depart from my orbits
of madness.

Leave my burning fields,
leave the smokes and its blackness,
let me be the candle
that burns to light your darkness,
then crucify my soul on your chest.
Don't cry for me, take me down,
bury me between your ribs
write on my head stone:
"A poet was laid to rest."
Every time the wind blows,
every time you touch a tree,
every time you hear the weeping of the grass,
every time you see a wave leaving its sea.
Don't cry for me,
sigh and remember
"Men do cry."

November 1992

"Man is by nature a political animal"

Aristotle

SILENCE

I'm still talking to the things
and the things still answering
with lies,
still counting the stars like crazy
from sunset till
the morning rise,
painting the tiredness
beneath my eyes.
I see ugliness,
another piece of me dies.
I think of the hungry children,
my heart cries,
I seek the truth in the
old books
but you must pay
the ultimate price.
I beg the wombs
to give me a newborn baby,
to mark the beginning
of our time.
O Lord,
Give me a sign
or a woman to bless the
falling of my rise.

June 1985

49

"There are three men, lovers of wisdom, lovers of honour, and lovers of gain"

Plato

THE EVENING BLUES

One evening, I felt so blue my heart was going to cry.
No friend around to talk to,
No soft shoulder to rest my head and sigh.
I said: "A drink in my old local
Might see my sadness go by."
I entered the place,
I ordered my drink and to the old,
familiar faces I was nodding my
head saluting them with a silent "Hi!"
In the very corner I sat,
I lit my cigarette and down in one, my drink was gone.
Man, I was so dry.
Another one, me old man, because I am still dry.
The only time I felt wet either by the Dublin rain
or my eyes when let to cry.
I turned my head; saw the moon.
Sitting alone, drinking Martini and seemed to be shy.
If I tell my story, the ignorant will say it's a lie
The dreamer will say, "it's drink talk",
The gentleman will excuse oneself and say good-bye.
The one who never possesses beauty will laugh,
The sad one will sigh, the wise man will smile,
The crazy will cry.
But if no one believed my story, I will die.

Dublin, 1989

"I'm a citizen, not of Athens or Greece, but the world"

Socrates

"Thus" - Sayeth the Lord

"Thus" - sayeth The Lord.
In the beginning
Was the word
And the word
was God?
We couldn't
comprehend it
so we invented
the sword.
The world was his
and it's not
"To be or not to be".
But be and it is.

2003

"Believe what you see and lay a side what you hear"

Arabic Proverb

Thy Eyes*

Your eyes in the moment
Of wakening,
Desirable lips
To the homeless a pillow.
Your eyes, sacred places
of warship.
Your eyes to the
Poet's
Inspirations
And two gazelles
In the moment of
Relaxation,
Your eyes are two pieces
From the night,
Two stars and
Two swans
Forever together,
Two silky curtains,
Fields of heather.
Your eyes are calling -
Come and never leave.
Your eyes are beautiful painting
Cross the sky
With Adam admiring Eve.

Benghazi 1983.

* I wrote the original poem in Arabic in 1983

"By night an atheist half- believe in god"

Edward Young

TRY

It's basic - try to understand
The things around me,
But it's the most complicated thing.
From the beginning
Of the creation of the Man, the word,
The concept of The Lord and the trees.
They said the clocks weren't ticking,
The time read zero and the world
submerged in silence.
No life.
Then the big bang, huge explosion,
The pendulum starts its revolution.
That's what they said, but deep in my heart
I knew that the seconds were ticking,
The sound and the echo,
The movement and the stillness
The beauty and the ugliness,
The Lord and the Devil,
The water and the fire,
The greed and desire,
The good and the evil.

"The Lord taught the man
The things they did not know"
With the pencil how to write,
With the mind how to read,
With the tongue how to speak.

He created the "mankind" from cloth
And the plants from a seed.
Some go backward
To search and seek what already is
In front of us.
Some go forward searching
For what already is behind us.
For all the knowledge we know
We only know little.
Theology,
Philology,
Philosophy,
The Lord is there, no doubt
Empty souls and mind drought
Leads to hallow and shallow shout.

December 2004

"He knows death to the bone-man has created death"

W.B.yeats

The Prophecy

How did he die?
I can tell how he lived.
She leaned over my wounded shoulder
Whispered in my ear
With a heavy sigh,
She drew a tear beneath my eye.
Before she turned to say good-bye
She was weeping with baby cry
I thought she will never
Let go of my hand,
My tear touched the face of Mother Earth
To bless the sand
To kiss its grains and ask
The heavens to start to cry
Wash the blood and give a sign of new beginning
In the wasteland.

I was alone,
Isolated, wounded, broken and manipulated
My steps felt heavier than stone.
The sorrow nested deep into the bone,
Sleepless eyes that never
Knew the break of dawn
Ugly souls, cracked moon
Ghost cities
Howling wind of cry and moan
Hungry children

Burning fields
State of fear, fortuneteller and blind seer
How did they come here?
With a big lie and colour of fear
How did he die?
I begged in vain.
It was a gloomy day
The colour of grey.
He walked to the gallows
Proud and tall,
Never rattled never crumbled
Never fell.

Only you, my son, to blame
You change your name from Saladin to James Bond,
You exchange your shield for a bottle of whiskey,
Your Arab horse for Cuban cigar,
Your mighty sword for western blond
Only you, my son, to blame
Geronimo fought but it was too little too late
Because he never knew how they play their dirty game.

Dublin.2007

*"The greatest glory in living lies not in never falling,
but in rising every time we fall"*

Nelson Mandela

" I was no chief and never had been, but because I had been more deeply wronged than others, this honour was conferred upon me, and I resolved to prove worthy of the trust"

Geronimo

Wall*

Every time we open our eyes
Every time we raise our heads
Towards the skies
To seek the light.
Every time we rise
Every time we speak
The truth, they change it
To horrible lies.
Every time we stand tall
Every time we reach with hands
Towards the sun
They build between us a mighty wall.
They fill the air
With the sound of guns
Every time we shout
"FREEDOM!"
They call us stupid and dumb
They send us to hell
And for those citizens
Home becomes a prison cell.

1984

*I wrote the original poem in Arabic in Benghazi 1984.

Bonjour

Bonjour good citizen,
What's your fate going to be?
A pillory or guillotine
My sadness follows me from
The River Liffey to the River Siene
As I passed the Louvre
Taking by it's beauty and splendour,
Touch of rain and voice of a singer.
I smelled blood
I passed the" Porte de Lion" and still linger.
Suddenly the ground swallows me
To the subway system
Escaping the big gates of the city.
Seeking a moment of peace to remember
Through the tunnels of pain
But the curse of Katrina Groshinova
Follows me every where, and I always
Miss my train.

16.07.2008

Paris

"You are the ruination of my country, no nation has the right to occupy another, we will never surrender, we win or we die as for me I will live longer than my hang men"

Omar Mukhtar

Tragedy of the River Euphrates

Stand a little by the River Euphrates
What do you see?
Helmets belong to soldiers who came
From faraway lands
Tarnished with rust
Stay a little longer
What do you see?
Rotten corpses of foreign soldiers
Covered with heap of earth
Sand and dust.
Just to be fair
Harden the stare
Try to remember
The good days of
Old and rare
When the moon gave the river
The colour of silver
And the shine of crystal
When the dates were
Pure and vestal.
Then came the cowboys
From Arizona, Texas and Denver
Stupid and crazy,
Blind and rude
They gave the river
The colour of red
And for red is the colour of blood.

Stand a little by the Euphrates
Where the giants of Arabia once stood
Don't vex your heart alone
Don't weep and moan
Keep the stare.
Speak with the voice of silence
Oh, my grief
This I cannot bare.

October 2008

"Justice is like a train that is nearly always late"

Yevgeny Yevtushenko

BEAST

In my chest
Blazing fire
With mighty desire
To fold up the sun,
Scatter the stars
Boil the earth
Beneath the feet of every liar.
Inside me mighty beast of words
Wants to kill
Swims in oceans of holy ink
Woe to those from my quill.

2009

ONCE UPON A TIME

Once upon a time
Long ago
On the first break of dawn
When the letters were created and
The first word was born
People were suppressed
Freedom was murdered under
The light of the moon.
Once upon a time, not long ago
There was beautiful places
We called them homes
They were loved by the children,
The women and men
They wrote to the moon
Love poems.
Lived just like the Sufis in their domes.
Suddenly everything was doomed
Bing, bang, boom.
Then came the storm,
Men, like the tartar, and the Mongol
Aggressive and fool
They burned everything-
The fields, the books
They shot at the pigeons
They cut all the trees
They can't tell the difference
Between evil and good,

Between child and machinegun,
A bullet and the rose,
Satan and The Lord
Suddenly the world submerged
In darkness
Everything was painted in the colour
Of gloominess
They crucify the freedom.
Humanity was murdered
By the swords of the sinners
Once upon a time
From here to eternity.
There will always be
Executioner and prisoner.

January 2007.

"Ever tried, ever failed. No matter, try again, fail again. Fail better"

Samuel Beckett

"If we value the pursuit of knowledge, we must be free to follow where ever that search may lead us. The free mind is not a barking dog, to be tethered on a ten-foot chain"

Adlai Stevenson

REFLECTION

Is that you?
Looking insane
Miserable and desperate
Like your head is under
The ruthless blade of the guillotine?
Why make excuses
When you know they are uglier than a sin?
Remember, only serpents
Change their outward skin
With the same type of expression.
Come here, don't be afraid
Bury your head between my bosoms, and
Let it rain, let it rain, let it rain
Wash your heart with tears of pain
Those that never get washed
Eventually will rust
Let the rivers wash away the human dust
Only now things will go silent
Remember in my face
There is a space
Little place, where your lips
Can embrace, even for a moment
The eternal peace
For lost souls
Of the human race.

2008

"I dream my paintings and then I paint my dreams"

Vincent Van Gough

REMEMBER

When I wonder away and
Remain sombre
When in times I say nothing and coil
Into my own inner-self,
Always remember in my silence
I love bigger
I love you in the moments of my sadness
I love you in the moments of my sanity
And in the days of my madness,
I love you forever.

August 2008

"When the rich wage war, it's the poor who die"

Jean-Paul Sarter

Exodus

Thousands of years into
The windward
A wanderer
Like the weeping willow
Walking in the corridors of
The gallows
Dreaming of soft touch and a pillow
Exhausted wounded but
Hopeful, easy and mellow
Returning to the land
Where the sun and the
Sand made of gold.
Where the treasures of
Wisdom are buried and thousands of
Secrets that have never been told.
Oh my grief, the eyes were painted
With sorrow, the streets were
Empty and narrow.
Peace was gone
Satan was the king
Their flag was of scowl and the colour of madness
They extinguished the sun
They told them darkness
Is sacred and hallow
Oh my grief, a thousand years
Seeking the truth
Thousand years a wanderer

The curse of the sparrow
Another thousand must follow.

September 2008

"Be the change that you want to see in the world"

Mahatma Gandhi

"If you tremble indignation at every injustice then you are a comrade of mine"

Che Guevara

CHE GUEVARA*

He passed through here
With the break of dawn.
I saw him with my own eyes
Hugging the moon
Kissing a bullet
Washing in the river
Telling his comrades
"Our victory is soon."
I saw his face
I kissed his forehead
I gave him water and bread
We spoke words that never have been said.
He walked like a giant
He wasn't followed either
He was led
I swear by The Lord.
I saw him standing but dead
Covered in red
In the deep of the night
Under the wing of darkness
I glanced at his killers
But suddenly they fled.
Moments before his death
Before taking his last breath,
I heard him saying:
"Continue the struggle
Don't give up the fight."

I can hear the songs of redemption
I can see the army of darkness defeated
By the morning light
I can see the pigeon's returning
To the skies of Havana
Blessing the fields of sugar and the harvest
Of mango and banana.

I saw him talking to a farmer
Kissing the forehead of earth
Flirting with the moon
Singing glory to freedom

Some times with tunes of
The sorrow of death
Sometimes with tunes of
The joy of birth.
I cried with grief
Along with the fields of Havana and
People from near and far
Bolivia sleeping without
The morning star,
Oh Guevara, you die brave
You die alone
No home, no loved ones
To say their final farewell
Nor a grave.
I saw him shaking hands with the trees
Kissing the grains of rain

Blessing the fields of wheat
Talking to the children
Hiding his pain.
It was sad day for me and victory for the jailer
I carried his frail remains
With my own hands
I carried him across the land
Till my legs could no longer stand.
I buried him at my wounded knee
I covered his corpse with
Leaves, branches and sand.
I wrote on his head stone:
"Here laid to rest, Chi - the revolutionary".

July 1976.

*I wrote this poem in Arabic in Benghazi in the summer of 1976.

"The media is the most powerful entity on earth, they have the power to make the innocent guilty and to make the guilty innocent, and that's power. Because they control the minds of the masses"

Malcolm. X

Abomination

I feel that the time of
Abomination is coming
Rising high the banners of
Hate and dissolution,
Sweeping everything that comes
Its way
Except the seeds that
Breathes the good and knows the road to God.
In the time of
Abomination,
Alone you will sing your poem,
Alone you live in isolated dome,
Alone you cry,
Alone you sigh,
Darkness will prevail
Alone you will sail.
Nothing
But the weeping of
The soul
And the seasons
Will be fall followed by fall.
In the time of abomination
Justice will be murdered
By the hand of indignation,
Alone you walk,
Alone you cry,
Alone you talk,
Alone you die.   *May 1984.*

"That is what learning is. You sudden understand something you have understood all your life, but in a new way"

Doris Lessing

FORTUNE-TELLER

This is what the fortune-teller
Said to me.
With a grin of surprise
While she was reading deep
Into my eyes-
"You are seeking the truth
But you can find only lies.
A million helmets, my son
Will land
In the city of Baghdad.
Soldiers coming from
Faraway lands.
They will paint the walls with
The colour of sadness,
They will drink the River "Euphrates"
In seconds
And turn everything
Into madness.
They will shoot
At every woman and every child,
Leaving them dead.
They will turn the earth into iron
And fill skies with lead,
They will raise the flags of abomination
And dissolution
So high
And shout with hatred: "Everyone must die!"

They will burn all the palm trees
And leave Iraq in mayhem and despair,
They will spread
Plague and fleas,
They will close the gates of the city
And throw away the keys.
I can see, my son,
The court of evil celebrating
With the drink of blood
And laughter of deceit

A minute before mid-night
On New Year's Eve.
But just before the dawn
A baby-boy will be born.
His name will be, Hope.
The name will echo in
Every corner of the globe.
In one hand he holds a sword,
In the other, an anchor and a rope."

Justice is his destiny
Sanity, fidelity, dignity
Are his Trinity.
He will wipe all the tears
And deliver the courage
That defeats fears.
The soldiers will be nothing;
Helmets without heads,

Bones which are long dead.
He will hug the city of Baghdad
And hundreds of millions of kids will shout
In jubilation
"Dad, dad, dad!"
And, my son, you will always be
The Sinbad
Who dreams of the lighthouses,
The shore, the sand
And the city of Baghdad.
It's late, I must go, my dear.
"Good-Bye"- I replied in a state of fear.
And from a little distance
She turned and shouted
"It's almost mid-night, my son,
Happy New Year!"
Oh Lord,
I hope it's soon
The rise of that dawn.

2004

"Rain, Rain, and hunger in Iraq"

Bdr Shaker Alsayab.

Tale about grain of rain

Between the grain of rain and a seed
Eternal love story
Based on need
Not in greed.
Between heavens and earth
Endless trade
Continuously
Provide us with
Water and bread.
Between a cloud and the wind
Spiritual marriage and
Violent love,
Every time they mate
They start with scream and
End with a cry.

2009

"The journey never ends as the soul is eternal"

Ali Hussein

Journey

When the night draws its curtains
When the world submerges in darkness
When the cafes close its doors
When the inns throw out the last of alcohol-loaded heads
When the streets are empty
When the wind blows across the universe
When the air is cold
When the voices echo with silence
The journey of loneliness begins
And my soul starts knitting the coats of sadness.

June 2009